About the Book

Robert E. Lee was a soldier and a patriot, as his father had been before him. Both fought bravely for the young country they loved, the United States of America.

But when trouble broke out between the northern and southern parts of the nation, Robert E. Lee had to choose a side. And although he believed slavery was wrong, he was loyal to his birthplace, the South. Lee became general of its army. And even though the South lost the war, people on both sides called him "one of the greatest American soldiers."

Robert E. Lee

by Ruby L. Radford
illustrated by Tran Mawicke

G. P. PUTNAM'S SONS

NEW YORK

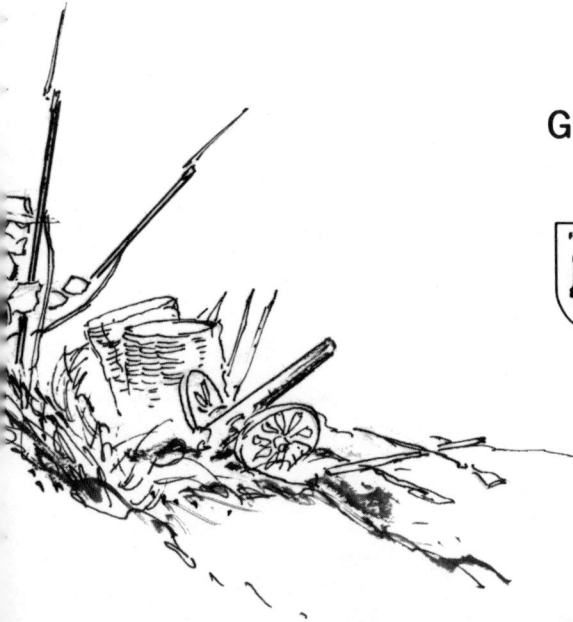

SBN: GB 399-60818-4
SBN: TR 399-20329-X

Library of Congress Catalog Card Number: 73-75829

PRINTED IN THE UNITED STATES OF AMERICA
07209

For "Rusty" Schumpert

Little Rob stood on the seat of the
carriage and waved. Tears filled his eyes.
He was sad to leave Stratford.

He had been born in the big house three
years before on January 19, 1807. His name
was Robert Edward Lee, but most people
called him Rob.

Rob loved the Virginia plantation with its woods, streams, and animals. Best of all he loved the horses. His big brothers, Carter and Smith, often took him horseback riding.

"Alexandria will be a nice place to live,"
said Rob's sister Ann. She dried the little
boy's tears. "The new capital, Washington,
is right across the Potomac River."

"There will be good schools in town," said
Carter.

"And stables for the horses right behind our new house," added Smith.

The carriage rolled on down the sandy road. Rob cheered up when they stopped by a stream to eat their meal. How he loved picnics!

Henry Lee

"It will be better to live in a small, warm house," his mother said. The large house at Stratford had been cold and dark.

Rob's father was General "Light-Horse Harry" Lee. He had helped General George Washington win freedom from English rule. He had also been governor of Virginia.

Soon after the Lees arrived, Rob began to like the new brick house in Alexandria. There was so much to see and do. Before long, too, Rob had a new baby sister, named Mildred.

General Lee took the children to see the
sights. It was exciting to visit the new
capital of Washington. One day Nat, the
coachman, took them in the carriage to see
Mount Vernon. It was George Washington's
old home.

Washington was one of Rob's heroes.
General Lee told many stories about the
first President of the United States. In a
speech, General Lee had once said
Washington was "first in war, first in peace,
and first in the hearts of his countrymen."

14

Rob's father told him, "Someday I hope
you will be a great leader like Washington."

General Lee was getting old. He owed
money to many people. Soon the family had
nothing to live on except some money left to
Mrs. Lee by her father.

When Rob was about six, his father was badly injured in a fight with a mob. He was never well again. Finally he went south to warmer weather and never came back again. He died when Rob was eleven.

Life was different for young Robert E. Lee
after that. His older brother Carter went off
to college. Smith joined the Navy. And their
sister Ann became very sick. She was sent
to a doctor in Philadelphia. Mildred was still
a little girl.

So Rob had to become the man of the
family. Much of the time his mother was ill.
He helped care for her when he came home
from school.

When Rob was fourteen, he went to
Alexandria Academy. Professor William
O'Leary taught him Greek, Latin, and
arithmetic.

Soon Mrs. Lee was too weak to see to the care of their home. Rob went to market for her. He helped Lulu, the cook, plan the meals. After school he would put Mrs. Lee into the carriage. Then Nat would drive her around Alexandria. During those hard days, Rob learned how to be gentle and kind to the sick.

By the time Rob was seventeen he had learned all Professor O'Leary could teach him. "I want more education," he told his mother. "But I know you have no money to send me to college."

"You must go to college anyway," she said.

She pulled a shawl closer around her shoulders and thought. At last she said, "Maybe you could get into West Point. The government would pay your expenses while you learn to be a soldier. That would have pleased your father."

"The examinations are very hard," said Rob. "But I can try."

He did study hard for the tests and was accepted at West Point. When he left home, his mother said, "I don't know how I can live without Robert. He is both son and daughter to me."

Robert rode on a paddle-wheel boat up the
Hudson River to West Point. He was now a
tall, handsome young man.

At first life seemed strange at the military
academy. The new boys had to sleep in tents.

They were awakened at dawn to march before breakfast. The rules were very strict. The boys could not smoke, drink, or play cards. They could be sent home for getting into a fight.

Robert studied hard. He did not get a single bad mark for breaking a rule while at West Point. He was graduated second in his class. Then he was called Lieutenant Robert E. Lee.

After graduation, Robert had to hurry home to his mother, who was very sick. She died that summer.

Robert's greatest comfort in his sadness was his friend, Mary Ann Custis. Soon she and Robert fell in love. Mary was the great-granddaughter of Martha Washington. The Lee and Custis families had always been friends.

Lieutenant Lee's first job in the Army was building forts, bridges, and highways. He was sent to Georgia to build a fort. Two years later he came home and married Mary Ann Custis.

Mary and Robert lived in her father's mansion, Arlington, in Virginia. Soon they had children. Sometimes Lee took his family with him when he went away to build bridges or forts.

In 1846 war broke out between Mexico and the United States. Both countries claimed the same lands. Lee had to leave his family at Arlington to go to fight. His youngest son, Robert, Jr., was only two years old. Lee wondered if he would ever see his baby boy again.

In Mexico Lee went ahead of the Army to
plan attacks. It was dangerous work. Once

he was in the jungle alone. He spied some
Mexican scouts. Quickly he hid under a log
that had fallen across a tree stump. Two
Mexicans sat down on the log to talk. Lee

thought his end had come. Ants and
mosquitoes stung him, but he did not move.
Finally the Mexicans went away.

35

Lee was in Mexico for more than two years. He became a captain, then a major. He did not see his family in all that time. Many times Lee and his horse, Grace Darling, were in great danger. She was struck by bullets seven times but lived.

At last the war was over. The Americans had won. General Winfield Scott, who led the Army, said that Lee was the "greatest military genius in America."

Lee was made a colonel. But how glad he was to go home! He rode Grace Darling part of the way. He also brought home a pony, Santa Anna, for Robert, Jr.

His little boy had grown so that Lee did not know him. When two young boys came into the room at Arlington, Colonel Lee grabbed and kissed the wrong one! But Robert, Jr., felt better when he saw his new pony.

Soon after Colonel Lee's return the Army sent him to Baltimore to build a fort. He took his family with him. In 1852 Lee was made superintendent of West Point. For three years his family lived there in a large stone house. There were stables for Grace Darling and Santa Anna.

Every afternoon Colonel Lee and Robert,
Jr., went riding. Lee was a fine horseman
and taught all his six children to ride well.

Then Mrs. Lee's father died and left the Arlington mansion to her. Colonel Lee got a leave of absence from the Army and took his family back home. During the next two years he repaired the buildings and ran the farm. Mr. Custis had ordered that all his slaves be freed in five years. Colonel Lee also thought slavery was wrong. He had no slaves of his own.

People in the North wanted all slaves freed. Southerners said they needed slaves to work in the cotton fields. They felt that each state should decide the slavery question for itself. Finally war broke out over states' rights and slavery.

Lee was sad when Southern states began
to withdraw from the United States in 1860.
When Virginia seceded, Lee was loyal to his
state. But it was a hard decision. "I cannot
fight against my own people," he said.

He left the United States Army. He took
off his blue uniform and put on the gray one
of the Southern Confederacy. Jefferson
Davis was its President.

Soon President Davis made Lee a general.
He put him in command of the Army of
Northern Virginia. So much riding was hard
for Grace Darling. Lee bought a stronger
horse and named him Traveller. Through

four years of war they were always together.
Some said that Traveller had a charmed life.
Bullets whizzed around him in battle but
never struck him. He was a noble gray horse
with black mane and tail.

Richmond, Virginia, was the first capital of the Confederacy. The Yankees from the North tried to capture it. Lee gathered 80,000 men to defend the city. But the Northern army was much larger.

"If they capture Richmond, our cause is lost," said General Stonewall Jackson, who had brought soldiers to help Lee.

"We will not give up," said General Lee
firmly.

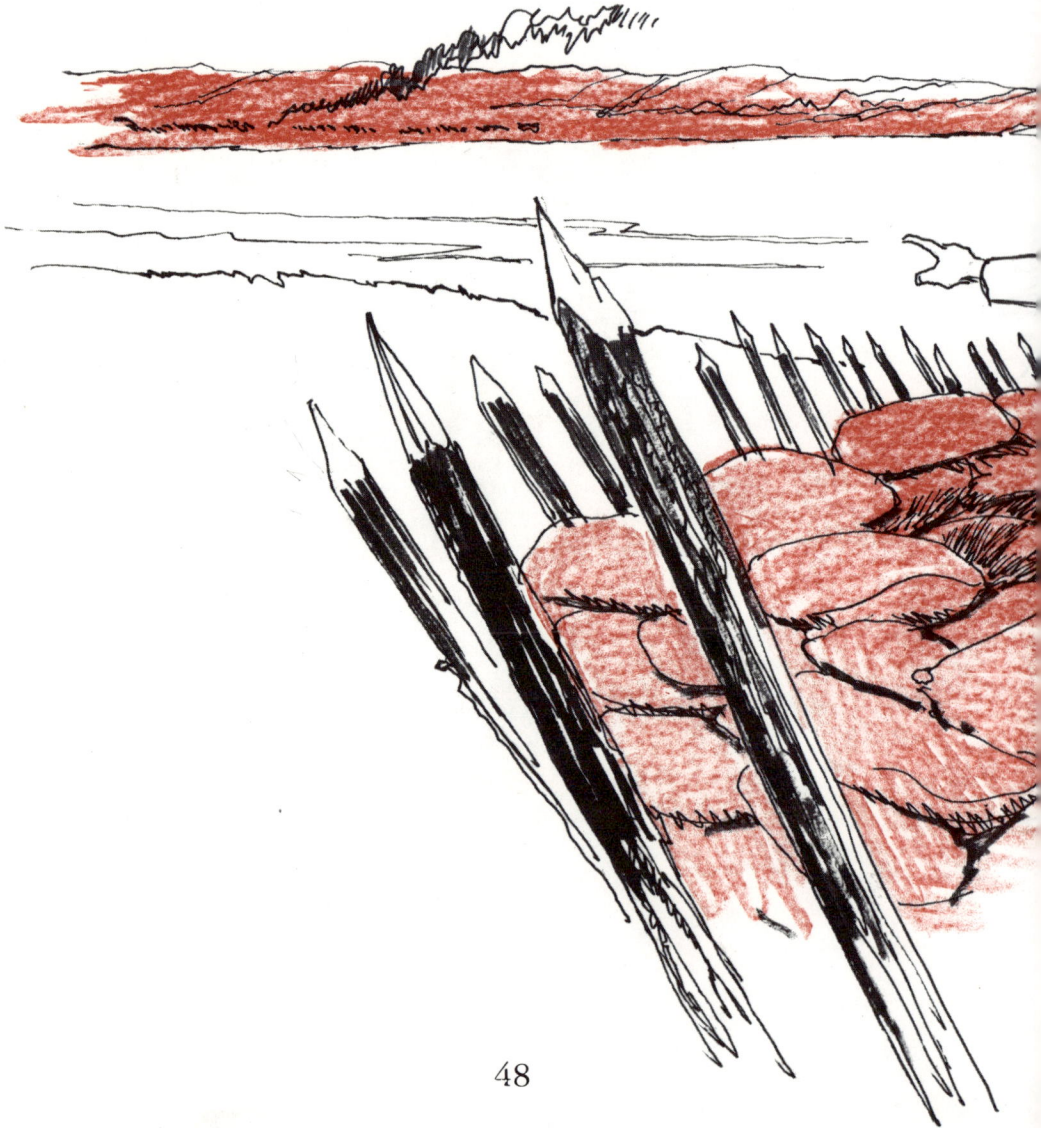

After a month's standoff the enemy
fled. Richmond was saved.

That was the first of many battles. Lee's
biggest defeat was at Gettysburg in
Pennsylvania. His army had moved into
enemy territory. But the Northern army was
too strong for them. Lee had to retreat.
Thousands of men and horses lay dead on
the battlefield.

General Lee's heart was sad at so much
suffering. In his tent at night he prayed for
the injured men. He visited them with words
of comfort. His men loved him so much they
called him Uncle Bob.

Between battles the men tried to rest in
camp. At night they sat around the campfires
and talked of home. General Lee worked on
battle plans in his tent. Often he could hear
his men playing on mouth organs and banjos.
They sang "Dixie" and "Bonnie Blue Flag."

For a while when they were in winter
camp Lee had a pet hen. Every day she laid
an egg on his cot. So each morning the
general had a fresh egg for breakfast.
Sometimes the little hen flew onto Traveller's
back. The beautiful horse always stayed just
outside the general's tent.

For four long years the war went on. Lee's sons were fighting also. But he saw little of his wife and daughters during those hard years.

Many sick and injured men had gone
home. The soldiers were now ragged and
hungry. There was not enough food for the
horses. The United States Army had more
money and men. At last, when the
Confederate Army was driven out of
Richmond, Lee knew their cause was lost.

He could not bear to see more of his men killed. He decided he had to give up.

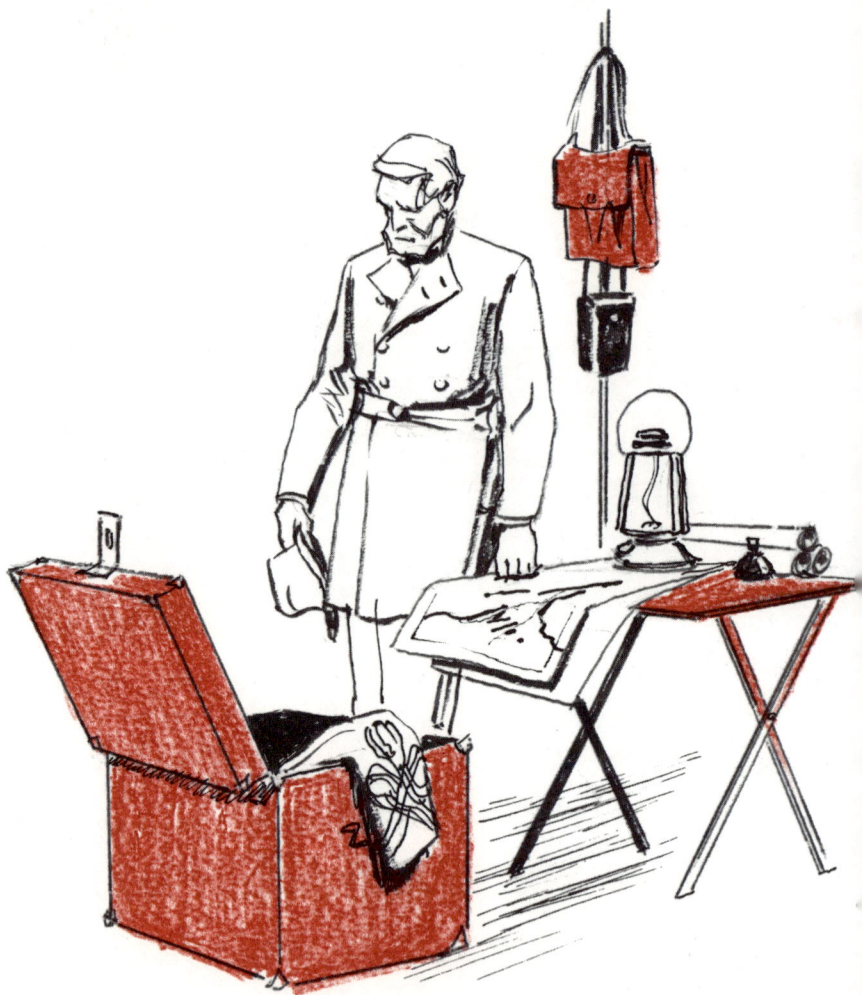

Dressed in his best gray uniform, Lee rode
to Appomattox. There he met General
Grant, commander of the Northern Army, at
a farmhouse. Grant was a kind victor. He let
Lee's men keep their horses. But he took
away their guns. He ordered food be sent to
the half-starved men.

Sadly Lee rode the tired Traveller back to
Richmond. Along the way people cheered,
even Lee's former enemies. People in the
North and South said he was one of the
greatest American soldiers. He was offered
many jobs.

Lee had lost everything in the war. He had
to start anew. After thinking about all his
offers, he decided to become the president of
Washington College in Lexington, Virginia.

During the rest of his life, he lived there happily with his family. He enjoyed being with young people and training them for peace, not war. The boys loved the old general too. Everyone greeted him as he rode by on the noble Traveller.

Finally the old man became too ill to go
out. He died on October 12, 1870. He was
buried in the chapel at Washington College.

Later the name was changed to Washington and Lee University, in honor of the two greatest generals of our country.

Key Words

academy

attack

capital

captain

carriage

claimed

colonel

command

confederacy

education

enemy

examinations

expenses

freedom

general

genius

governor

graduated

lieutenant

major

mansion

military

plantation

retreat

scouts

secede

slavery

stables

superintendent

territory

The Author

Ruby L. Radford was the author of almost fifty books for children and young adults. She also contributed numerous short stories to magazines and wrote several plays for television. Until her death, she made her home in Augusta, Georgia. She was the author of *See and Read* biographies of Sequoya, Robert Fulton, Dwight D. Eisenhower, and Mary McLeod Bethune, all published by Putnam.

The Artist

Tran Mawicke was born in Chicago and educated at the Chicago Art Institute. He has worked as a free-lance artist in New York City since 1935 and is a past president of the Society of Illustrators. Previously, the artist illustrated a *See and Read* biography of Zachary Taylor for Putnam. He makes his home in Bronxville, New York.